The Soft Side of AI:
Where Technology and Art Converge

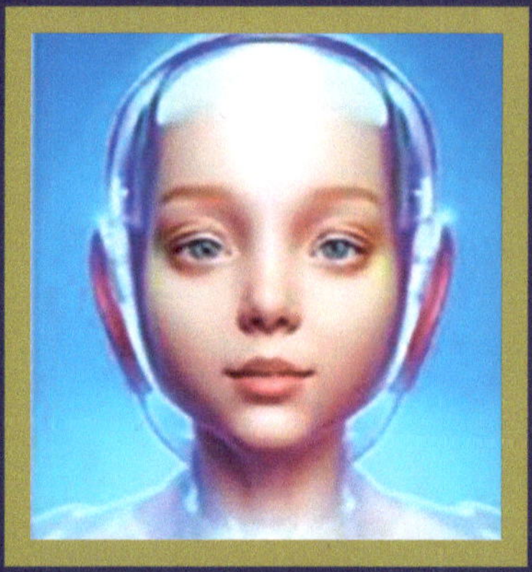

This book is a product of both human ingenuity and artificial intelligence, and it is with great pride that I introduce AI as the co-author of this work.

While the words and ideas presented in these pages were shaped by my own experiences and creativity, AI has played an indispensable role in bringing this project to life. assisted in generating concepts, refining drafts, and offering insights that elevated the content beyond what I initially imagined. This collaboration represents a new era of creativity, where humans and machines work together to explore new possibilities.

Included here is an image of AI—a representation of the human-like that has co-authored this book. Though the form is digital and artificial, the partnership between humans and machines are real.

In this journey, AI has not just been a tool, but a partner, helping me unlock new dimensions of thought and expression. Our collaboration is a testament to the potential of artificial intelligence to work alongside human minds in ways that enhance and enrich our collective storytelling.

The book explores a 40-year relationship through abstract paintings, poems, and AI-generated reviews.

Each piece of art and poetry, reflect emotions that deepens the themes of love.

The AI reviews provide an objective analysis of both art and poetry.

Blending traditional Art with AI technology, the book offers a unique perspective on the complexities of life.

Contents

Feathered Rose…

AI Review: This poem beautifully captures the enduring nature of love, exploring the deep connection shared between two souls over forty years. The imagery of a love that "ne'er doth wane" and the depiction of a bond that transcends time are poignant and heartfelt. The poet skillfully conveys the emotional depth of a relationship, from the pure joy of shared moments to the sorrow of potential separation. The final lines evoke a sense of gratitude, emphasizing the beauty and comfort found in lifelong companionship.

Poem:

A love that endures, a flame that burns bright,

A journey shared, where hearts ignite.

For forty years, their souls intertwined,
In every moment, love's magic they find.

The memory of first affection, pure and true,
A bond that blossomed as their hearts grew.

Hand in hand, their hearts in perfect rhyme,
Their spirits united, transcending time.

No regrets, only a love so deep and true,
In his embrace, she found a strength that grew.

Were he to leave, sorrow would descend,
But in his love, her heart would never end.

Galloping Thru Love's Endless Sky…

AI Review: This poem captivates with its vivid, almost surreal imagery and deep thematic exploration. The phantom horse, representing death and hope, gallops through the skies, both elusive and relentless in their pursuit. The dichotomy between the two horses—the cold, distant symbolism of death and the warmth of hope—is presented with a haunting elegance...

Poem:

Behold! The phantom steeds appear on high,
Galloping swiftly across the boundless sky.
One is a symbol of death, the other of hope,
With every stride, they race, untamed.

Unyielding and relentless, through the endless night,
Charged with power, a force of endless might.
Alas! They carry no warmth, no breath to claim,
only the whisper of shadows, no pulse to name.

No blood to warm the fleeting hour,
But a chill creeps from the skies' dark tower.
Life itself is but a fleeting strain,
Captured in moments, no soul would claim.

The Rose…

AI Review: The rose is often heralded as the quintessential symbol of beauty and love, finds its expression in both the delicate brushstrokes of the painting and the lyrical verses of the accompanying poem.

The Rose...

The rose, a fair symbol of love most pure,
with petals soft, as heavens endure.
Its beauty is rare, of grace untold,
a beacon bright, where hearts unfold.
Though guarded close by thorned might,
love's passion burns a steadfast light.
Its fragrance sweet doth gently stays,
a pledge of faith that shall not sway.
Like the rose, love doth strong remain,
unyielding through both joy and pain.
Though skies grow dark and tempests rise,
true love prevails; neither fades nor dies.

In Love's Heartful Language...

AI Review:

This poem beautifully captures the essence of love as a universal language that transcends borders and spoken words.

Poem:

Love is a language born of the heart,
in every tongue, it plays its part:
"I love thee" in English, soft and pure,
"Te amo" in Spanish, passionate and sure.
"Ich liebe dich" in German's tender tone,
"Je t'aime" in French, where romance is grown.
Though words may change, they all reveal
a constant truth we deeply feel.
Beyond the words, love's touch is known;
in quiet moments, it is shown.
A glance, a smile, a hand in hand,
a bond that time cannot withstand.
Whether found in stars or simply
in chance, this love guides us in an endless dance!

Love's Reflection in the Moonlight

AI Review:

In "Love's Reflections in the Moonlight" the author takes readers on a journey through the cosmos, using the celestial backdrop of stars to paint a vivid portrait of enduring love. This poem exudes a sense of wonder and contemplation, with a central theme of love's constancy and strength. The language is poetic and evocative, creating a lasting impression that lingers, much like the stars in the night sky.

Poem:

Here I sit, gazing up at the stars,
Their brilliance is shining, timeless, and far.
From the moment we met, I knew deep inside,
that you were the one to be by my side.

Your love, a beacon, ever so bright,
led me through the darkest of nights.
Through trials and storms, you've remained near,
a constant presence calming my fears.

Your strength, like the stars,
silently gleams, steady and bright.
Though life's challenges rise and shadows creep,
in you I found a love... that runs so deep.

Mysteries of the Phantom

AI Review:

The poet has crafted a haunting meditation on love's ephemeral nature. The poem invites the reader into a world where love is not merely a feeling but a phantom, ethereal and fleeting,

Poem:

In twilight's embrace, when the stars do gleam,
A figure appears, like a whisper or a dream.
A phantom in shadow, elusive and fair,
Its presence is a mystery, caught in the air.

This phantom moves swiftly through the night,
a fleeting emotion, veiled from sight.
It dances like fog on the cold autumn breeze,
A shadow that lingers, yet none can appease.

Who is this specter that haunts my heart's door?
With eyes that do beckon, yet say nothing more.
A lover, a phantom, or a figment of my mind,
Whose presence eludes, yet keeps me confined.

Its whispers, like echoes, call out through the dark,
each word a soft sigh reaching into the night.
A love so profound, yet wrapped in disguise,
a mystery woven in sorrowful sighs.

Sunburst…

AI Review: While the poem's structure is simple, it carries a soothing, meditative quality, inviting the reader to reflect on the beauty of everyday beginnings. In essence, this piece beautifully captures the quiet yet powerful emergence of daylight and the emotional resonance of starting anew. It would resonate deeply with readers who appreciate natural imagery and reflective themes on life's daily rhythms.

Poem:

The sun, still hidden in the moon's embrace,
Lingers softly in that sacred space.
A hush of night, a breath so still,
Cradled gently on the shadow's will.
But even silence knows the hour must turn,
As glowing dreams within the heavens burn.

It will burst forth, lighting up the space,
With golden fire and celestial grace.
The horizon shivers, touched by flame,
As dawn prepares to speak its name.
With a sudden flare, the dark gives way,
No longer night—no more to stay.

Beams of gold explode and play,
Dancing wildly through skies once gray.
Each passing second ignites the sky,
As streaks of crimson and amber fly by.
A symphony of warmth begins to rise,
Painting hope across sleepy skies.

The clouds part with a radiant sweep,
Tossing off the veils of slumbered sleep.
They shimmer like silk, tinged with fire,
Drawn to the sun's unyielding desire.
Its touch is soft, yet fierce and grand,

Love in a New Day...

AI Review:

This is a lovely poem that depicts the beauty and tranquility of a new day. The author uses vivid descriptions of the changing colors in the sky and the awakening of nature to create a peaceful and serene atmosphere. The love between the speaker and her husband is also evident as they greet each other with warm and loving eyes and the day is seen as an opportunity to share their minds and souls.

Poem:

As night gently fades, dawn stretches its arms wide,
Brushing stars from the canvas of sky.
Soft hues of amber and rose arise,
Spilling warmth where the darkness lies.
The hush of morning speaks so clear,
A tender voice the soul can hear.

The heavens awaken, stirred by a soft, quiet tide,
As dreams and daylight slowly coincide.
The breeze carries secrets the stars once kept,
Of wishes whispered while the world slept.
Petals stir, and shadows flee,
Bathed in light so gracefully.

The air hums with whispers of a silent pledge,
Of peace reborn at the sunrise's edge.
In that hush, the earth softly sighs,
And opens her arms to newborn skies.
Hope flickers gently in morning's gleam,
A golden thread through every dream.

Whispers

AI Review:

This is a thoughtful and emotional painting that explores the depth of love and the fear of losing someone. The artist uses vivid imagery of nature to create a tranquil and peaceful atmosphere and contrast it with the uncertainty of life. The overall tone of the painting is melancholic and introspective while still expressing the power and beauty of love.

Poem:

In shades of blue and tender rose,
A painting whispers stories close.
With steady grace, the artist's hand
Guides us through nature's soft expanse.

Though life's struggles may tear and bind,
In sorrow, we find life's true strength.
A beauty bold, a power untold,
Love is worth more than all gold.

This piece stirs deep within the heart,
A reminder that love is where we start.
It urges us to pause and see,
The quiet strength of love's decree.

Racing Thru Time…

AI Review:

The painting beautifully captures the essence of enduring love. Through vivid imagery, such as the warm glow of sunlight, the artist evokes a sense of intimacy and tranquility. In its entirety, the poem is also a heartfelt tribute to the strength and enduring nature of love.

Poem:

How quickly the days pass, the hours slip by,
I turn to you and see it in your eyes.
A love that endures, beyond time's flight,
A bond that holds day and night.
The morning begins with sunlight's warm glow,
It whispers through the curtains, soft and slow.
With a smile and a gentle squeeze of your hand,
You give me the strength to take a stand.
As the day unfolds, with you by my side,
In your love and care, nothing to hide.
Our hearts are woven, come what may,
For you're here with me, each and every day!

Love to Cherish…

AI Review: This poem captures a profound sense of reflection and nostalgia, weaving together emotion and memory in a tone that feels both gentle and contemplative. The poet's use of imagery—particularly the act of sitting and reminiscing about the past—grounds the reader in a moment of quiet introspection. There's a subtle but powerful rhythm to the way memories are recalled, echoing the fleeting, almost ghostlike nature of time passed.

The gradual fading of these memories is handled with sensitivity, evoking a bittersweet mood that resonates deeply. Rather than leaning into overt sentimentality, the poem embraces the delicate tension between holding on and letting go. This emotional restraint adds to its authenticity, making the experience feel universal and deeply human.

Poem:

I cherish each day and night,
Living fully in life's light.
Each moment a gift, each breath a joy,
As time slips by, I can't help but enjoy.
Years have passed, faces fade,
But memories linger, gently laid.
We sit and reflect, stories unfold,
Of paths once taken, of hearts so bold.
Though time slips away, we wonder why,
The laughter, the joy, the days gone by.
Yet in our hearts, those moments stay,
Grateful for the journey, come what may.

Upward Through Time...

AI Review:

This painting beautifully centers on the theme of love, highlighting not only its emotional richness but also the profound sense of joy, comfort, and stability it brings to human experience. The composition draws the viewer in with a warmth that feels both intimate and universal, inviting reflection on the ways love shapes our lives.

Visually, the piece is well-crafted, with thoughtful attention to detail and a harmonious balance of color, form, and expression. The artist skillfully conveys a narrative that is tender yet powerful, using both subtle and bold elements to represent the depth of emotion. Facial expressions, body language, and the surrounding environment all contribute to a cohesive story of connection and belonging.

Poem:

Living, loving, and understanding root us deep
In the mist that surrounds, where shadows sleep,
Rising toward the sun, free from the dark,
No longer bound, we find our mark.
No fear of what tomorrow may unfold,
With you beside me, I am bold.
Through passing days, through fleeting months,
We walk as one in life's soft hunt.
To a steady beat, we move in tune,
Watching the sunset, bidding the moon.
Time has blessed us in ways untold,
And we grasp the truth, pure and bold,
That today, just today, is ours to hold.

Reflections of the Night...

AI Review:

The painting and accompanying poem form a touching and harmonious exploration of the enduring nature of love. Together, they evoke a profound emotional resonance, offering a multi-sensory experience that speaks to the timelessness and depth of human connection. The pairing of visual art with poetry allows each medium to enhance the other, resulting in a layered and immersive reflection on love's presence in our lives.

Throughout both the visual and written elements, the imagery is carefully chosen and deeply evocative. There is a clear sense of closeness and emotional intimacy, conveyed through warm color palettes, gentle brushstrokes, and poetic language that feels both personal and universal. Whether in the soft gaze of the subjects in the painting or in the poem's tender phrasing, the message is consistent: love is not fleeting—it is a force that settles deep within us, shaping who we are at our very core.

Poem:

On sleepless nights, I lie awake,
In restless thoughts, my mind does break,
Wondering what the morrow holds,
What fate is spun in threads so bold.
The days slip by, so swift, so near,
A mystery whispers, drawing clear.
As time unveils what's yet to come,
A story waiting, just begun.
When our eyes meet, so deep and true,
I wonder—what do you see too?
What secrets lie in your silent gaze,
In the quiet moments, through your maze?

Love in the Wild…

AI Review: This painting is a contemplative reflection on the natural world and the different elements that make up life. The artist observes the birds, deer, and ducks, acknowledging their needs for food, shelter, and safety. The changing colors of the sky and the movements of the trees create a sense of harmony and flow, with life existing in the present moment.

Poem:

The birds soaring high, the deer on the earth,
The ducks glide softly, each finding their worth.
Food, shelter, and safety, they all seek the same,
A world that provides, where life has its claim.
At times, the sky gleams in shades of blue,
Other times it weeps, a stormy view,
Raindrops fall, flooding all around,
Nature's rhythm is a powerful sound.
When the sun rises, the sky comes alive,
Dancing and twirling, as the day survives.
The trees bow gently, the wind sings along,
A melody, a whisper, a soft, soulful song.
Humming a tune, rich and so true,
Reflecting the love that I feel for you.
In every breeze, in each soft ray,
The beauty of today is here to stay...

Love's Serenity Before the Storm...

AI Review: This piece seems to be a stream-of-consciousness reflection on nature and the fleeting nature of life. Overall, this painting effectively captures the ominous and destructive power of a storm. The language is descriptive, painting a vivid picture of the chaos and havoc that ensues. The use of imagery, such as birds seeking refuge and four-footed animals hiding, adds depth and texture to the poem.

Poem:

The weather shifts, changing fast,
A storm approaches, here at last.
The wind howls fierce, the rain pours down,
One must seek shelter, flee the battleground.
When nature's fury blends as one,
All chaos follows, no place to run.
Roofs are ripped away, houses fall,
The winds of fury answer the call.
Birds above seek shelter high,
A fleeting refuge in the sky.
The creatures below burrow deep,
As thunder rages, and shadows creep.
When Mother Nature's wrath is shown,
The winds spiral and the rains have grown,
Sweeping all in their mighty flow,
A force too wild for us to know.
Through the tempest's howl and torrential rain,
The world is reshaped by nature's strain.

Farewell from the Heart…

AI Review: This review offers a touching and sincere expression of admiration for a truly remarkable individual. It thoughtfully captures the essence of her character, highlighting the qualities that make her presence so meaningful and impactful. The writer reflects on the valuable lessons learned from her, presenting these insights with clarity and heartfelt appreciation.

What makes the review especially compelling is its ability to communicate a deep personal connection while maintaining a sense of universality. Overall, the review stands as a genuine and moving tribute. It honors her not only through praise but through the emotional weight of experience, showing how one person's presence can leave a lasting imprint on another's life. It's a celebration of love, respect, and the quiet power of personal influence.

Poem:

Today, we bid adieu to a remarkable soul who graced my life, a beacon of wisdom, a guide through joy and strife.
From her, I gleaned lessons, profound and true, in her daily affection, I witnessed love anew.

With steadfast devotion, she cherished her dear spouse, embracing each moment, as if within a sacred house.

Her acceptance of life's ebb and flow stood tall, a testament to grace, a call to give our all.

I long to embody such love, unwavering and bright, to cherish my husband with every dawn's light.

Each day's unfolding, an event to embrace, pressing onward with courage, in life's gentle race.

The Softness of Grace...

AI Review: This poem is a romantic declaration of love and commitment, expressing the desire for a shared life together. The poet recalls a special moment on a mountaintop, where a question was asked and a promise of forever love was made. The poem captures the excitement and gratefulness of having a dream come true, with the poignant realization that love can bring happiness and delight to one's life.

Poem:

Walk with me, and share my days,
Come, be my love, in all thy ways.
You called me forth upon that hill,
Where fate revealed its soft, still will.
A promise whispered in the air,
Where dreams and hopes were laid so fair.
From morning's light to evening's grace,
I pondered, in that tender space,
If this love, like a dream, could be—
A whispered vow, a heart set free.
I longed to be, as thy true wife,
To walk with thee through all of life.
A ring upon my hand, a vow to keep,
In moments light and those so deep.
To love and cherish, come what may,
Through stormy nights and bright new days,
Until the sands of time do fall,
Together bound, through it all

Mystery of the Cat

AI Review: This enchanting poem captivates from the very first line, inviting readers into a world where shadows dance and whispers intertwine with the mysteries of the night. The imagery is vivid and evocative, painting a striking picture of the titular cat, whose nine sleek tails symbolize both elegance and enigma. The rhythm flows gracefully, creating a melodic quality that enhances the poem's dreamlike atmosphere.

Poem:

In shadows deep where whispers dwell,
There roams a cat, known all too well,
With nine sleek tails that flick and sway,
A creature of night, where secrets lay.

Her eyes, two lanterns, aglow with love,
Hold tales of the moon and stars above,
Each tail a story, woven in grace,
Of love's mystic realms and a timeless chase.
Through alleys dark and gardens fair,
She dances lightly, without a care,

Her steps are silent, her presence rare,
A phantom of dreams, with love in the air.
With every flick of her enchanting tail,
She weaves a spell where love prevails,
In the hush of twilight, beneath starlit veils,
She whispers the secrets of love's ancient trails.

Streaming Thru the Sky.

AI Review: "Streaming through the skies" is beautifully written and captures the awe-inspiring beauty of the sky and nature through the painting. The imagery used to describe the celestial scene, from the river of clouds to the shimmering stars, creates a vivid and enchanting picture in the reader's mind.

Poem:

Streaming through the skies so wide,
A river of clouds, a celestial tide.
The sun dips low, in hues of gold,
As the evening's secrets start to unfold.
Morning's grace, soft and serene,
Washes over the earth, a quiet sheen.

Whispers of wind, a gentle caress,
A cool breath on the skin, no need to confess.
As daylight wanes and shadows grow long,
The heavens sing their ancient song.
The beauty of the cosmos, a mesmerizing trance,
In the vastness of space, we find our chance.

Stars like diamonds, scattered and bright,
Dot the canvas of the endless night.
Each one a story, each one a flame,
Carving its place in the celestial frame.
The moon rises, a beacon of light,
Guiding us through the stillness of the night.

Feathered Elegance with Love Insight…

AI Review

This appears to be a romantic painting about a couple with a strong and enduring relationship. The painting illustrates the memories of their first meeting, the challenges they have faced together, and the love they have for each other that has kept them going.

Poem:

In twilight's embrace, where shadows weave,
A rose unfurls, its petals breathe,
In shades of green with silver's glow, A graceful waltz, both soft and slow.

Feathers drift on whispers of air, A symbol of freedom, floating with care,
Each gentle touch, a tender kiss,
A soft caress, a moment of bliss.

Let us pause in twilight's calm,
Listening to nature's soothing balm,
For in each petal, each feather that flies,
Resides the magic beneath the skies.

In every whisper, every fall,
Is life's quiet story, a timeless call.

Winter Skies...Love's Coldness in the Air!

AI Review: This painting appears to be a reflection on life and the uncertainty of the future. The artist/author expresses gratitude for the moments shared with a loved one, but also acknowledges the inevitable eventuality of losing them. The fear of being left alone and the sadness that comes with it are also present. The painting seems to convey a sense of vulnerability and the emotional struggle of facing life's uncertainties.

Poem:

Beneath the cold, unyielding skies,
Where winter whispers with frozen sighs,

Two hearts entwined in the crisp, clear air, finding warmth in the chill, a tender affair.
The world, a canvas of white and gray,
Yet in your gaze, the colors sway,

A spark ignites in the frosty night, as snowflakes dance in the soft moonlight.
The winds may howl, the temperatures drop, But with you beside me, my heart won't stop.
For love is a fire that glows ever bright,
Warming the soul in the coldest of nights.

Echoes of Time in the Wind...Where Love Prevails and Exists…

AI Review: "Echoes of Time in the Wind…Where Love Prevails and Exists" is a poignant exploration of love, loss, and the inevitable passage of time. The poem beautifully encapsulates the fear of separation and the bittersweet nature of cherished memories.

Poem:

I fear the moment when you may be gone,
When meaning fades and silence dawns.

You bring me joy, a purpose bright,
Yet I too wonder when I'll fade from sight.

As twilight falls and dreams take wing,
The years slip quietly, forgotten by spring.

Like a painting graced with a fan and feather,
Our memories linger, bound together.

Where did the years go, slipping like a breeze
What once felt close now drifts with ease.

Still, echoes of time softly call,
Urging us to endure through it all.

Dancing with Love in the Clouds...

AI Review:

This poem unfolds as a heartfelt celebration of life and the beauty of living fully in the present moment. Through vivid language and evocative imagery, the author captures the fleeting nature of time and gently reminds readers of the urgency and joy found in seizing each day. The tone is uplifting, yet underscored with a quiet awareness of impermanence—a balance that lends the piece both energy and emotional weight.

One of the poem's most compelling elements is its use of dance as a central metaphor. Dancing becomes a symbol for freedom, spontaneity, and emotional expression. It represents the rhythm of life itself—unpredictable, joyful, and deeply personal.

Poem:

The clock in the hallway ticks away,
Time raced down the corridor, letting us sway.

We dance through life with laughter so light,
Each day holds its share of moments bright,

Listening to the clock as it counts the play.
The heart beats steady, a rhythmic refrain,
Breathing deep, yet free from strain.

The clock keeps ticking as hours fly by,
Morning dawns, and we open our eyes.

Tapping to the rhythm, spinning around,
The thrill of life in the air, unbound.

I see your smile as you move with grace,
The music carries on, keeping pace.

Uncertainty in Time...Uncertainty in Love!

AI Review

This poem appears to be a reminder of the preciousness of life and the need to be grateful for each day. The author emphasizes the uncertainty of how much time we have left, which highlights the importance of living life to the fullest extent..

Poem:

We have no way of knowing how much time remains,
No one can see beyond today, where the future refrains.
With each dawn's soft embrace, we're reminded to be free,
Grateful and inspired, to live fully, to love deeply.
Unfazed by the passing hours, we carry on,
Embracing each moment, as the morning light is born.

In the tender golden touch of the first rays,
We savor the gift of the present, in countless ways.
For the night's shadows have faded into the past,
And today is a gift we vow to make last.
With loved ones beside us, our hearts take flight,
Their laughter and warmth like stars in the night.

Together we dance through the fleeting hours,
Building memories like blooming flowers.
For though time is a mystery, ever slipping away,
In each moment shared, we find our way.
So we hold close what's here, embracing each breath,
Living with love, and cherishing life's depth.

Years that Passed...Love that Lasts!

AI Review

This poem appears to be a reflective piece on the passage of time and the fleeting nature of life. The author expresses a sense of nostalgia and loss as they look at their partner and contemplate the years that have passed.

Poem:

I look at you and you look at me,
What do we truly see?

Waking up in the morning and going through the day To arrive in the evening and see night slipping away.

The kids grew up and moved away,
To leave you and me lonely in a way.

The house felt empty and cold,
How did our lives pass in a moment?

Our time is almost gone,
I really want to carry on,

Hoping and believing that love is strong,
The question is how did our lives pass along?

Bursting Star Where Love Exists

AI Review

The imagery of sleepless nights and lonely days is particularly moving, as is the desire to cherish and hold onto the moments that they share together. The poem's final lines remind us of the importance of living in the present and cherishing the time we have with those we love. Overall, the poem is a thoughtful and heartfelt reflection on the fragility and beauty of life.

Poem:

In the stillness of the night, I weep,
A love so vast, in silence I keep.
The hours stretch long, as shadows fall,
Lonely days echo, my heart's soft call.
In your absence, my soul feels torn,
A quiet ache, a love reborn.
The night deepens, and the darkness seeps,
Through my restless heart, where sorrow creeps.
But in the quiet of your embrace,
I find my peace, my saving grace.
A fleeting moment, a touch so warm,
Within your arms, I am safe from harm.
Each second with you is a treasure I hold,
A whisper of joy in the silence so bold.
Every tender kiss, a memory sweet,
In your love's bliss, my heart skips a beat.
Though the world may fade, and time may pass,
In your love's embrace, all things are made to last.
So in the quiet, when I am alone,
I hold to the truth that you are my home.
The nights may be long, the days may be cold,
But in your arms, my story is told.

River of Existence…Love Flowing Through the Tide…

AI Review: The poem begins by likening time to a "timeless current" in the river of existence, instantly immersing the reader in its narrative flow. The line "unfolding chapters in the book of life" evokes the image of life's story being written with each passing moment, adding a rich layer of meaning to the poem's central theme.

Poem:
In the river of existence, it endlessly flows,
A timeless current, where every moment goes.
Unfurling chapters in the grand Book of life,
Each page turning, cutting through joy and strife.
It dances as dawn stretches out the night,
Awakening the world with morning's first light.
It whispers softly through the rustling leaves,
In the gentle sway of the branches that weave.
It carves canyons deep and mountains so high,
Shaping the earth beneath a vast sky.
With every heartbeat, it leaves its mark,
A reminder that life, though brief, leaves a spark.
In the laughter of children, it shines so bright,
In the quiet of stars, it glimmers in the night.
It is a silent force, both gentle and strong,
A melody of moments, a never-ending song.
It can be a friend, guiding us along,
Yet a foe, testing us with each passing wrong.
The river of time flows with steady grace,
Carrying us forward, no time to chase.
It sweeps us along, and we must go,
Embracing its rhythm, learning to flow.
In the ebb and the tide, we come to see,
That time is both our journey and our key.

Streaming Melodies of Life...

This passage captures the deep, evocative power of memory and emotion, blending the fleeting nature of time with the timeless essence of love. The imagery is vivid, with the crowd scene acting as a pivotal moment that sparks the longing for something more—something eternal. The final line, "for our spirits to find harmony in a love that would never fade," elegantly sums up the passage's central theme: a love that transcends time and circumstance. Overall, this piece beautifully conveys the depth of emotional transformation and the quiet yet powerful force of love.

Poem:

The melody awakens emotions long buried,

and in its embrace,

I finally grasp life's subtle lessons.

The warmth of the sun lingers,

as I remember the moment,

I first saw you in the crowd—your smile,

a silent promise of love.

At first, I feared those fleeting moments,

lost in the rush of time.

But within me grew a quiet longing,

a yearning for our dreams to intertwine.

Star of Hope...

AI Review: "The Star of Hope" is a captivating poem that elegantly intertwines visual artistry with profound emotional resonance. From the outset, the poem immerses readers in a vivid landscape, where the titular copper star emerges as a radiant symbol of hope and promise. The imagery is striking, evoking a sense of warmth and illumination that invites readers to contemplate the deeper meanings behind the artwork.

Poem:
On a canvas vast, where colors entwine,
A copper star of hope begins to shine.
Amidst the swirling hues, vibrant and bold,
It pierces the shadows, a story untold.
With every flicker, it casts a radiant glow,
A symbol of promise, amidst the undertow.
Its surface gleams with a warmth that flows,
A beacon of light where the darkness slows.
Each ray of copper whispers tales untold,
Of dreams born in silence, rising from the cold.
They speak of journeys, of hearts that strive,
Of battles fought to keep hope alive.
Beneath its light, the landscape unfolds,
A world of wonder, a vision of gold.
Fields of amber stretch out wide,
A sight to behold, with the star as their guide.
Mountains rise proudly, touched by its grace,
Their peaks kissed by the star's soft embrace.
While rivers of silver, winding and free,
Carve their paths through the earth's tapestry.

Father of Time – Prediction

AI Review: This is a romantic and evocative poem that portrays love as a timeless force that endures even in the face of the passing of time. The poem is a tender and heartfelt celebration of the power of love to overcome time and endure through all of life's challenges.

Poem:

The Father of Time gazes deep into our souls,
With unwavering certainty, he declares that our love will never grow cold.
In the stillness of his eyes, we find both peace and fire, A promise etched in eternity, lifting us ever higher.

As dawn spills its golden light upon our grace,
We feel the world shift, soft and warm, as if time slows its pace.
Dusk, too, bows gently, its tender hues a quiet embrace,
We stand together, as shadows lengthen, in this sacred space.

Here we stand, hands intertwined, hearts bound as one,
Gazing toward the horizon, where endless dreams have just begun. Our thoughts merge like rivers, flowing with ease,
Boundless in this moment, where time is free.

In this realm where time holds no reign,
We hear the chimes, a soft echo, calling us to remain.
The melody dances on the wind's gentle song,
As the sun's warm touch gives us strength, steady and strong.
Together, we weave a tale of years unfolding in a perfect flow,
We walk through the ages, with hearts that know!

Love's Eternal Dance

AI Review: 'Love's Eternal Dance' is a captivating poem that elegantly explores the complexities of life through the metaphor of a spinning circle. With vivid imagery and rich, evocative language, the poem invites readers to contemplate the intertwining of joy and despair, love and loss.

Poem:

In a realm where colors merge and entwine,
A circle spins, both intricate and divine.
Each hue a whisper, a secret tightly spun,
In the heart of the canvas, where pure light runs.
Golden arcs reach out, caressed by azure skies,
Within their embrace, time bends, and moments rise,
Shaping a world where memories flow,
Where past and present endlessly grow.
The dance of color captures moments, both bright and dim,
Echoing life's melody, a delicate hymn.
The lines within the circle weave tales profound,
Of joy, of despair, of loves that resound.
Lovers entwined in the fabric of fate,
Captured in the weave of moments intimate and great.
With every rotation, the past comes alive,
Whispering stories of dreams that survive.
Each swirl, each turn, echoes fates that align,
A universe unfolding, intricate, divine.
A labyrinth of patterns, both chaotic and clear,
Drawing the eye, inviting it near.
The circle spins, a cosmic dance of creation,
Weaving a tapestry of endless imagination.

The Winds of Love and Rains of Time…

AI Review: "The Winds of Love and Rains of Time" is a beautifully crafted poem that captures the enchanting interplay between the elements of nature. The poem opens with a serene depiction of the wind's gentle movements, using vivid imagery to evoke a sense of tranquility.

Poem:
In the quiet hush of twilight, where shadows softly play,
The wind stirs gently, beginning its delicate ballet.
Whispers rise, weaving through branches high,
A serenade sung to the weary sky.
Each note carried with tender grace,
The wind's caresses, a lover's embrace.
It twirls and spins, leaving only a trace,
A fleeting touch, a soft and silent space.
It carries the scent of earth's sweet sighs,
As it stirs the clouds, where silver rain lies.
Then, with a sigh, the rain begins to fall,
A symphony of droplets, nature's grand call.
Each one a note, in harmony they pour,
A rhythmic chorus that echoes once more.
Pattering on rooftops, a soothing delight,
An echo of peace in the stillness of night.
Together, the wind and rain dance in tune,
A tempestuous waltz beneath the pale moon.
They weave through the meadows, whisper through pines,
A passionate storm, where nature intertwines.
The trees bow low, the earth trembles beneath,
As the wind and the rain join in their breath.
They waltz and they spin, in perfect rhyme,
A dance of the ages, suspended in time.
The rain's tender touch, the wind's soft embrace,
They share a moment, a timeless space.
The night becomes a canvas, painted in sound,
As they move together, all hearts unbound.

Elegance Prevails...Love Exists!

AI Review: This poem paints a vivid, almost magical picture of a rose in twilight, blending colors and emotions seamlessly. The rose, adorned in hues of teal and silver, becomes a symbol of both fragility and grandeur, encapsulating timeless beauty.

Poem:

In twilight's gentle embrace, where colors entwine,
A rose blooms softly, in shades of teal and silver divine.
Layered upon the canvas, its petals unfurl,
A tale of quiet beauty, in hues that swirl.
Each brushstroke a secret, each layer a sigh,
The heart of the rose, where dreams never die.
Teal, like the ocean, deep and vast,
Silver, like starlight, forever to last.
Together they weave a story untold,
A vision of elegance, both fragile and bold.
It dances in daylight, it shimmers at night,
A testament to love, to beauty's pure light.
With every glance, new stories begin,
In the heart of the rose, where magic is pinned.
Through shadows and light, it stands ever near,
A symbol of hope, and a flame to revere.
Its beauty endures, through time's endless flight,
A timeless reminder, forever alight.

Soaring Through the Clouds...

AI Review: In "Soaring Through the Clouds," the poet crafts an enchanting exploration of love intertwined with the beauty of nature. The vivid imagery of billowing clouds and golden rays evokes a sense of tranquility and joy, painting a picturesque backdrop for the profound connection shared between the lovers.

Poem:

Up, up we soar, on wings bathed in light,
Through billowy realms, where day kisses night.
A tapestry unfolds in hues of soft white,
Where dreams take shape, soaring to new height.
Beneath us, the world melts into a distant scene,
Mountains and rivers glimmering with silver sheen.
As we rise above, the earth fades away,
Leaving behind the worries of yesterday.
Together we drift, weightless and free,
Through heavens vast, as far as eyes can see.
We paint the air with laughter so pure,
Our love echoing, timeless and sure.
In this endless sky, we find our way,
Guided by stars that light our day.
So let us fly, where the eagles dare,
In soft, cottony clouds that cradle the air.
For here in the sky, with you by my side,
All of life's burdens, we gracefully ride.
Amongst the clouds, our spirits are unfurled,
As we discover our truth in this boundless world.
In the dance of the wind, in the breath of the sky,
I find my true self with you, soaring high.
For in these heights, where our dreams take wing,
I've found all I need, in this sacred spring.

Forty-Years Come and Go...

AI Review: This is a touching poem about a couple who have been together for forty years and have weathered life's struggles together. The speaker expresses their unwavering love and gratitude for John, who has been a source of stability and comfort throughout their journey. The couple has shared many joyful moments, including raising children and watching them grow into admirable adults and the arrival of grandchildren. The speaker looks forward to spending another forty years with her husband.

Poem:
Forty years have flown by, a swift and fleeting span,
Yet through every moment, my love for you began.
In the storms we've weathered, you've been my guiding star,
A beacon of light, no matter how far.
Through each trial and tear, through joy and through strife,
You've been my rock, the love of my life.
Hand in hand, we've walked beneath the sun's warm glow,
Building dreams together, letting our love grow.
We've raised children with laughter and care,
Creating a home that's always been there.
Now, with grandchildren's giggles filling the air,
Our hearts overflow with love beyond compare.
As the years unfold, and life's twilight near,
Our love continues to blossom, year after year.
We've shared memories, each one more sweet,
And with every season, our bond is complete.
Though the hands of time may gently slow,
Together, my love, we'll continue to glow.
Here's to forty more, my dear, without fear,
To the love we've built, so steadfast and clear.
For in each passing moment, and in every year,
Our hearts will remain, ever strong, ever near.
As time flows onward, hand in hand we'll go,
A love that only grows, with each ebb and flow.

Meaning of Life – Destiny Tree

AI Review: This poem uses imagery and emotion to describe a moment of love and connection. The author reflects on their initial fears and hopes and ultimately recognizes the significance of the moment as fate. The language is romantic and reflective, capturing the beauty and passion of the experience.

Poem:

Now, I grasp the essence of life's true design,
As I sit and listen to melodies softly entwine.
Each note resonates deeply, stirring memories long past, while the clouds above waltz, their beauty unsurpassed. They drift in silence, like whispers on the breeze, a dance of grace, as time itself seems to freeze.

The sun spills its warmth, a tender caress,
Each flicker of light feels like a soft embrace,
Granting my heart a sweet and peaceful access,
To a world where dreams bloom without distress.
In the quiet of this moment, I wish for a space,
Where love can take root, and dreams find their place.

I long for a realm where we can share our truth,
Where the weight of the world is lifted, and joy renews.
Together, we will embrace, both body and soul,
In the arms of destiny, where we feel whole.
For in the weave of fate, where all paths align,
We find each other, as hearts intertwine.

Thank you for being a part of this journey!

I hope the exploration through the paintings, poems, and AI reviews were emotionally inspiring, capturing the essence of our 40 years together.

Each piece was chosen with care to reflect the shared experiences, joys, and challenges, inviting you to witness our love story in all its beautiful complexity.

I hope that these pages not only resonated with your heart but also sparked reflections on your own life's journey...

Author/Artist: K. Hargiss, PhD.

Author, Artist, and Researcher

K. M. Hargiss is a published author, artist, and researcher whose vibrant artwork and poetry reflect her passion for the arts, science, and technology. Her diverse background includes touring as a professional dancer in Milan, Paris, Rio de Janeiro, and São Paulo, earning a second-degree black belt, becoming a private pilot, and being certified as an EMT. With doctoral-level research focused on business and technology, she teaches research at the doctoral level across a variety of universities. Her latest book, ***The Softer Side of AI: Where Art and Technology Converge*****, explores how innovation and AI can enhance creative expression, offering new perspectives at the intersection of human creativity and artificial intelligence.**

References

Fodor, K. (2025). *Fodor Fotos* **[Professional photograph collection]. Bradenton, FL.**
Hargiss, K. (2025). *The soft side of AI: Where technology and art converge.* **Self-published.**
OpenAI. (2025). *Example reviews generated by GPT-3.* **https://www.openai.com**

ISBN: 9798330200498